KIN

by Max Dickins

SAMUEL FRENCH

samuelfrench.co.uk

Kin was first produced by Suzanna Rosenthal for Something for the Weekend, and previewed at the King's Head Theatre before premiering on 2 August 2018 at the Belly Button, Underbelly, Cowgate, at the Edinburgh Festival Fringe 2018, with the following cast:

CAST
In order of appearance

SARAH	Abigail Burdess
LILLY	Kate Alderton

CREATIVES

Director	Oliver Senton
Producer	Suzanna Rosenthal
Set Designer	Simon Scullion
Sound Designer	Alex Johnston

CAST

ABIGAIL BURDESS
Sarah

Abigail Burdess' TV includes: *Cuckoo* (BBC3), *Fresh Meat* (C4), *Watson and Oliver* (BBC2) and the BAFTA-winning *That Mitchell & Webb Look* (BBC2).

Radio comedy includes: *Lobbyland, Before They Were Famous, Vent, Concrete Cow* and *Abi Hour* for BBC Radio 4.

Radio drama includes: *The Death of Grass, Publish and be Damn'd* and *Friends Like These*.

Stage includes: the British Comedy Award nominated tour of *The Two Faces of Mitchell and Webb*. Abigail is also a stage, radio and TV writer and 'supremely talented comic' *Time Out*.

KATE ALDERTON
Lilly

Kate Alderton trained at LAMDA, starting her career in Ken & Daisy Campbell's 24-hour play *The Warp*.

Recent credits include: *Cosmic Trigger* and *The Mycelium* at The Cockpit; *British Enough* at Birmingham Rep; *The Woods* and *Foolish People*; award-winning films *Armageddon Gospels* by John Harrigan and *The Elder* by Jacqueline Haigh.

Other credits: *The Pleasure Principle* at Tristan Bates Theatre; *Peepshow, Frantic Assembly, The Boy Who Left Home* and *The Tempest* at ATC; *Charley's Aunt* at Sheffield Crucible; *Powderkeg*, at The Gate; *The Warp* and *What The Butler Saw* at Theatre Royal Bath and *Going Straight* for Bill Kenwright. She played regular Anna Lacey in *Noah's Ark* for ITV. Kate is a performer and producer with The Mycelium.

CREATIVES

MAX DICKINS
Writer

Max started his career as a radio presenter for Absolute Radio, where he was nominated for a prestigious Sony Radio Award. He then turned to stand-up, performing thousands of gigs on the comedy circuit and creating three full-length solo shows for the Edinburgh Festival Fringe, including *My Groupon Adventure*, which was a sell-out at the Pleasance in 2014. His first book, *My Groupon Adventure*, inspired by that show, was published in June 2016. Max's first play *The Trunk* was critically acclaimed and named by *Theatre Weekly* as one of their top ten theatre shows of 2016. His 2017 show *The Man on the Moor* enjoyed a sell-out run at the Underbelly before touring nationally. *Kin* is his third play.

OLIVER SENTON
Director

Oliver directed Max's first two plays – *The Trunk* and *The Man on The Moor* (also UK tour) – for Edinburgh; and *Joan, Babs and Shelagh Too*, Gem Rudd-Orthner's play about Joan Littlewood and her circle which toured all over the UK. Also: Sartre's *The Respectable Prostitute* and Berkoff's *Harry's Christmas in London*; *Decisions, Decisions* for Snap Theatre in Colchester, *Love's Labour's Lost* and *The Tempest* for Mountview, *Romeo and Juliet* for Rose Bruford, and several plays for the Scene & Heard children's charity (including the launch of The National Theatre of Scotland at The Queen's Hall, Edinburgh). He is also an associate of Slung Low, a founder member of *Showstopper! The Improvised Musical* (Olivier award for Best Entertainment 2016) and of 'hard bardic' extemporisers, *The School of Night*.

SIMON SCULLION
Set Designer

Simon trained at Wimbledon School of Art and was a finalist on the Linbury Prize for Theatre Design. Work as designer includes *Peter Pan Goes Wrong* Tour and Apollo Theatre, Strindberg's *The Father at the Belgrade Coventry*, *Out There on Fried Meat Ridge Road* by Keith Stevenson at the Trafalgar Studios, *Quartermaine's Terms* Tour directed by Harry Burton, *Killer Joe* at The Edinburgh Festival, *Perdition* by Jim Allen at the Gate Theatre and *Showstopper! The Improvised Musical* at the Apollo Theatre.

ALEX JOHNSTON
Sound Designer

Alex has been working across all aspects of theatre and performance since graduating from LIPA in 2011. He works regularly as a Sound Designer, Lighting Designer, Production Manager and Chief Electrician in London, across the UK and further afield. He especially likes unusual and challenging projects, particularly site-specific work, work in found-spaces and work in unusual locations. Recent projects include *We Are Lightning* – MAYK (Production Manager), *KIN* – Barely Methodical Troupe (Technical Manager), *Sweet Tooth* – Elaine Mitchener (Lighting Designer), *Flood* – Slung Low (Chief Electrician) and *Yvette* – China Plate Theatre (Production Manager).

KIN

by Max Dickins

SAMUEL FRENCH

samuelfrench.co.uk

Acting Editions

BORN TO PERFORM

Playscripts designed from the ground up to work the way you do in rehearsal, performance and study

---

Larger, clearer text for easier reading

Wider margins for notes

Performance features such as character and props lists, sound and lighting cues, and more

---

+ CHOOSE A SIZE AND STYLE TO SUIT YOU

STANDARD EDITION

Our regular paperback book at our regular size

SPIRAL-BOUND EDITION

The same size as the Standard Edition, but with a sturdy, easy-to-fold, easy-to-hold spiral-bound spine

LARGE EDITION

A4 size and spiral bound, with larger text and a blank page for notes opposite every page of text – perfect for technical and directing use

---

LEARN MORE samuelfrench.co.uk/actingeditions

MUSIC USE NOTE

Licensees are solely responsible for obtaining formal written permission from copyright owners to use copyrighted music in the performance of this play and are strongly cautioned to do so. If no such permission is obtained by the licensee, then the licensee must use only original music that the licensee owns and controls. Licensees are solely responsible and liable for all music clearances and shall indemnify the copyright owners of the play(s) and their licensing agent, Samuel French, against any costs, expenses, losses and liabilities arising from the use of music by licensees. Please contact the appropriate music licensing authority in your territory for the rights to any incidental music.

USE OF COPYRIGHT MUSIC

A licence issued by Samuel French Ltd to perform this play does not include permission to use the incidental music specified in this copy.

Where the place of performance is already licensed by the PERFORMING RIGHT SOCIETY (PRS) a return of the music used must be made to them. If the place of performance is not so licensed then application should be made to the PRS, 2 Pancras Square, London, N1C 4AG.

A separate and additional licence from PHONOGRAPHIC PERFORMANCE LTD, 1 Upper James Street, London W1F 9DE (www.ppluk.com) is needed whenever commercial recordings are used.

IMPORTANT BILLING AND CREDIT REQUIREMENTS

If you have obtained performance rights to this title, please refer to your licensing agreement for important billing and credit requirements.

AUTHOR'S NOTE

Kin, started with a question. A question that had been niggling me for a while. When we say we love our family, what does that actually mean? Because it's not the same love we feel for our romantic partners, and if it isn't that, what exactly is it? So at the heart of this play is a love story between two sisters. It's a story about siblings, therefore. I have both a brother and sister. I know from experience that siblings have a unique and often tempestuous relationship. Depending on the day of the week, your sibling can be your best friend or your greatest enemy. Love and hate are tightly helixed.

It isn't just simple rivalry. (Although that no doubt exists.) It's much more complicated than that. The psychotherapist Dorothy Rowe, an expert on sibling relationships, says the central cause of tension between siblings is each's ability to 'annihilate' the other. In short, your sibling knows you so well that, whether by word or deed, they can destroy your sense of self in just a moment. This is because the idea of who we are as individuals doesn't just exist in us, it exists in relationship to other people. Specifically in relationship to how they treat us. Most people will indulge our version of who we are out of politeness. But siblings will happily trample all over it, whether they mean to or not. After all, your sibling knows exactly who you are. Or at least they *knew* exactly who you *were.* But that's another story.

On a more mundane level, siblings tend to be excellent at taking the piss out of each other. And therefore I've endeavoured to make this play funny. I hope I've succeeded. This play needs humour. It's too bleak without it. However I urge you to make the comedic moments your own. The set-pieces I've written are diving boards not strait jackets. If I was vain enough to offer you advice, which I clearly am, it would be this: aim to make these moments as truthful as possible. How did *your* mum dance? Also try to make them as specific as you can. How *exactly* did she dance? It's wise to follow Steve Martin's dictum that a comedian should be 'abnormally fond of the precision which creates movement'. All author's notes need a pretentious quote, and so now I've ticked that particular box I'll bid you goodbye. I look forward to watching your production.

Max Dickins, July 2018

ACKNOWLEDGEMENTS

I am sure it will be no surprise to you that putting on a play requires the input and hard work of a large number of people. I have been lucky to work with a talented bunch. Firstly, I'd like to thank Oliver Senton, the director, for his warm encouragement and insightful feedback as I developed the script. And not least for his work in the rehearsal room once it was finished. He brought the best out of everyone. The cast – Abigail Burdess and Kate Alderton – also brought great vigour and intelligence to their roles. My words seemed to have more heft in their mouths: it was a thrill to see. Then there is the producer, Suz Rosenthal and her team at Something for the Weekend who made all of this possible. Simon Scullion and Alex Johnston deserve plaudits too, they worked wonders with a small budget. Finally, I am – as ever – indebted to Kelsey Richards: you are a wonderful script editor; to Naomi Petersen: your notes have helped so much; and to the many actors who were involved in readings at various stages. Thank you to you all for helping me realise my vision for this piece. I'll never forget it.

This is for my agent, Becky Williams.

Thank you for all the inspiration.

CHARACTERS

SARAH – the eldest sister. Mid-late forties. City girl. Power haircut.

LILLY – the younger sister. Mid-forties. A mother. The air of an art teacher about her.

This script went to print during rehearsals and may differ from the text in performance

ACT ONE

This is dusty Midwest America. Idaho maybe? We're inside a humble bungalow. It's remote. In a small, rural town which is even more remote. The middle of nowhere.

As the audience enter, a local American radio station plays. A mix of cheesy DJs, silly American ads about car lots, and old rock songs. Perhaps there is a radio on stage, lit by a light?

The stage is split into two rooms. There is a door between the two. One is a small bedroom. In the bed is a body. We can't see his face, but we know he is there. In the adjacent living room, near the front of the stage, is a small round kitchen table surrounded by four chairs.

When the lights come up LILLY *(mid-forties, English) is standing facing* SARAH *(mid-late forties, English) on opposite sides of the room.* SARAH *has her luggage next to her. The show opens with an awkward silence between them that we sense has started before the lights go up. It should be as long as anyone can bear.*

SARAH It's not what I expected. This place.

LILLY No?

SARAH I thought it would be bigger.

LILLY Right. Well. This is it.

A pause.

SARAH It's very clean.

LILLY It wasn't clean when I got here.

SARAH Right. Well...well done.

A pause.

LILLY I like your dress...

SARAH Oh. This thing. It's ancient.

A pause.

You look well.

LILLY Do I? Oh. Thank you. *(Beat)* So do you.

SARAH I don't know about that. It was a long flight.

A pause.

You've changed your hair.

LILLY Have I?

SARAH Yeah.

A pause.

It's nice. Lovely style. Like you've not really made an effort.

LILLY Thanks very much.

SARAH No. I meant that in a good way.

LILLY It was a compliment?

SARAH Yeah. As in. The style... It's informal. Relaxed. Like you've spent no money on it at all –

LILLY It was quite expensive, actually –

SARAH *(trying to be nice)* No. That's what I mean. *(Beat)* It's like the 'just got out of bed look' men like to have now. It actually takes a lot of effort to look so lazy...

A pause.

LILLY Decent flight?

SARAH Fine. Yeah.

A pause.

LILLY Watch any good films?

SARAH I watched a documentary about Josef Fritzl.

LILLY Right.

SARAH *pulls a bottle out of a bag.*

SARAH I brought some champagne. Picked it up in duty free.

LILLY Champagne? I didn't realise we were celebrating. Is this a celebration?

SARAH I don't know. Do you feel like celebrating?

LILLY I don't know.

A pause.

He won't drink it.

SARAH He always loved champagne! The flash bastard. Any excuse. Well he called it champagne. It was usually...

LILLY Lambrusco.

SARAH Yes!

LILLY Sarah. He has days to live. Maybe hours.

SARAH Look. I came as fast as I could...it's just...

LILLY Work?

SARAH Yeah. Work. And...

LILLY Yeah.

SARAH I didn't know...

LILLY I understand...

SARAH I didn't know whether I wanted to come at all.

A pause. **SARAH** *puts the bottle of champagne down on the sideboard.*

I thought he had a dog? Or have I made that up?

LILLY A terrier. Yes. I've shut him in the kitchen... We'll have to decide what we do with it. We'll have to decide what we do with everything.

SARAH Let's split everything down the middle. Including the dog.

LILLY You should have the dog.

SARAH What does that mean?

LILLY Nothing.

A pause. LILLY *sits down. Returns to sorting a load of papers into two piles.*

SARAH How are the kids?

LILLY Fine. Thank you.

SARAH Thirteen and nine, aren't they? Tricky age.

LILLY They're sixteen and twelve.

SARAH Tricky age.

A pause.

Still living in Stroud?

LILLY Yes. No reason to leave.

SARAH The world is bigger than Stroud you know.

A pause. SARAH *goes to sit down, irritably brushing hair from the seat first.*

I fucking hate dogs.

LILLY You used to *love* them.

SARAH You've remembered that wrong.

LILLY When Dad brought Bruce home you didn't sleep for a week! You *adored* him.

SARAH Until he bit me. He bit my leg. Took a chunk out. I've still got the scar. Don't you remember that?

LILLY It wasn't his fault.

SARAH It wasn't his fault? He fucking bit me!

LILLY He was a rescue dog. He'd been through a lot.

SARAH Dad had him destroyed. He had to after that. I suppose.

LILLY He might have changed.

SARAH No. The die had been cast. That dog was a cunt. *(Beat)* Where does he keep the booze? I need a drink...

LILLY He keeps the hard stuff in the cabinet.

> **SARAH** *goes to pour herself a drink. Scotch. Far too big.*

SARAH I bought him some fags too. Silk Cut. Nice fat brick.

LILLY Sarah! He's got cancer!

SARAH Not lung cancer.

LILLY He was oddly proud of that. Like he'd proved the medical establishment wrong. Like he'd won.

SARAH *(pulling out a cigarette)* If cancer isn't a good excuse to have a fag I'm not sure what it is. Do you mind if...?

LILLY Not indoors.

SARAH Christ. You've changed.

LILLY Are you drunk?

SARAH What?

LILLY Are you? Are you drunk?

SARAH No.

> *Another pause.*

So...do we have a time frame?

LILLY What do you mean?

SARAH As in...do we know when he might die?

LILLY It's hard to be precise about these things.

SARAH Right. *(Beat)* Ideally he'd die by Friday.

LILLY Ideally?

SARAH I've really got to get back for a meeting.

LILLY Of course. Yes. Sorry. One second.

As if shouting to her dad.

'Dad, if you wouldn't mind getting on with it...Sarah's got to get back.'

SARAH I didn't mean it like that. This is a hard time to leave work for me. OK? The worst...

A pause.

LILLY Do you want to see him?

SARAH Is he awake?

LILLY No.

SARAH Is he conscious?

LILLY In and out.

SARAH I'm nervous.

LILLY Nervous?

SARAH I'm not good at small talk.

LILLY It's not a cocktail party Sarah.

SARAH I can't chat unless someone's talking back... It was bad enough when he was healthy. He'd ring me up on Christmas Day and we'd dry up.

LILLY He called you on Christmas Day?

SARAH He'd call me twice a year. Christmas Day. And on FA Cup Final day. Weirdly.

LILLY You were always his favourite.

SARAH Don't say that.

LILLY You're going to have to help me turn him in a minute. Otherwise he gets bed sores. *(Beat)* I will warn you that his balls are very swollen.

SARAH Lilly!

LILLY What?! They are. His balls are very very swollen. *(Beat)* And his scrotum's *massive*. *(Beat)* You could stick a pole under it and camp.

SARAH *shoots her an appalled look. Short pause.*

SARAH Where's the TV?

LILLY He doesn't have a TV.

SARAH He doesn't have a TV?! This is America. There should be fifteen fucking TVs... What are we going to *do*?

LILLY I don't know. Have a conversation?

A pause.

Dad's been talking a lot about the past. When he's been awake. He's been talking about Mum.

SARAH Where do you sleep?

LILLY I'm sorry?

SARAH Where do you sleep? There's only one bedroom...

LILLY I sleep in there...

SARAH You sleep with Dad?

LILLY No. Not *with* him. I'm on the floor next to him. On a lilo. *(Beat)* He gets frightened at night. He doesn't like to be alone.

SARAH Perhaps I should check into a hotel. Sleep there.

LILLY There's no need.

SARAH It's no big deal. I don't mind.

LILLY There's really no need.

SARAH Motels are so cheap –

LILLY You can sleep on the sofa.

SARAH I've already made a reservation somewhere.

LILLY You might miss it.

SARAH Miss it? I've just got here.

LILLY Dad could die any minute. I think you'll want to be here. Sleep on the sofa.

SARAH I need a shower. Christ. I stink. Do you mind?

LILLY Let's turn Dad first.

SARAH Yes. Of course.

LILLY Seriously – his balls are like grapefruits.

SARAH Lilly you are absolutely obsessed!

Both sisters laugh.

LILLY *(moving towards* **SARAH***'s bags)* Come on then. Let's get you settled. I'll help you unpack. I've got some photos of Tom and Sammy on my iPad if you want to...?

SARAH Yes of course.

LILLY I've told them a lot about Auntie Sarah.

Then **LILLY** *moves to embrace her sister with a hug.* **SARAH** *evades her.*

SARAH I'm sorry.

LILLY It's fine.

SARAH I'm not... I'm not ready for that.

LILLY I understand. I shouldn't have... I'm sorry.

SARAH Can't the nurse turn him? Isn't that her job?

LILLY How do you know it's a she? A woman. Could be a man.

SARAH But I bet it's a woman. Isn't it?

LILLY You always used to correct me on that. Do you remember? You used to tell me that *'pronouns create our reality'*.

SARAH Did I? Christ. I sound insufferable.

LILLY You were inspiring, actually.

SARAH Isn't it her/*his* job to turn Dad? He's paying enough.

LILLY Not anymore. When he declined treatment, when he decided he was ready to die, that voided the insurance. We get a state nurse for an hour a day. We could go private but it's $500 a day –

SARAH I'd pay a lot more than that not to see Dad's balls.

LILLY Dad thought it was a waste of money.

SARAH So you've been doing everything?

LILLY I don't mind... But he's heavy, so if you could help...

SARAH Jesus Christ. Look at this art work. He's done this place up like an Indian restaurant.

LILLY Dad never had much taste.

SARAH No. Mum had all the taste.

LILLY Have you been getting my letters?

SARAH His cactus is dead.

LILLY Have you though?

SARAH How has he managed that?

LILLY Because you never reply.

SARAH They can survive in deserts...

LILLY Did you at least receive them?

SARAH Look. This isn't easy for me. Being here. You know? It's hard. It's fucking hard, actually.

LILLY So you have read them?

SARAH Do we have to do this now? I've just arrived. Can this not wait? I don't want to do this now.

LILLY There isn't much time. We need to talk. Don't you think?

SARAH Not now. Please. Not in front of Dad.

LILLY Have you received my letters?

SARAH I don't want to play happy families. We've never been a happy family. Not before Mum died. Certainly not after.

LILLY Why are you here then?

SARAH Isn't it obvious?

LILLY I haven't seen you for *twenty years*. Why have you come now?

SARAH Duty. I'm here out of duty.

LILLY That's all?

SARAH My decision to come here... It didn't come from my heart. Or my brain, actually. It's not logical. Me being here. It came from this amorphous third place... Somewhere deep inside me. Which says that this is the right thing to do...

LILLY But you don't want to be here?

SARAH No. I don't *want* to be here. I don't *desire* to be here. I'm compelled to be here. Through some weird primitive response –

LILLY That's all family is to you? Some primitive response?

SARAH Isn't that what everything is?

LILLY No. Some things are built through will. Faith. Pulled together by the power of an idea.

SARAH And isn't family *an idea?* A biological imperative. That's *become* a superstition. This infallible holy grail...

LILLY You wouldn't say that if you had one.

SARAH And here we are: worshipping at the altar of family. On the deathbed of someone who ripped ours apart. He stands for the opposite of everything you believe.

LILLY Luckily for you I believe in forgiveness.

SARAH Saint Lilly lives on, I see. Must be exhausting. Carrying around that halo.

LILLY You seem ambivalent about dad dying. Like you're almost looking forward to it.

SARAH It would honestly affect me more if my cat died.

LILLY What a fucking awful thing to say.

SARAH He's already dead to me. He left, I mourned, I moved on. This is an apparition. Soon the ghost will leave and things will go back to how they were.

LILLY You want things to go back to how they were? *(Beat)* This is our chance. This is it. We need to talk.

SARAH I don't want to talk.

LILLY Why are you here then?

SARAH Duty. I told you.

LILLY I don't believe that. You're too stubborn. Too selfish. To be driven by duty alone.

SARAH Lovely to see you too.

LILLY Why did you come?

SARAH If we're not going to move him. I'm going to have a shower...

LILLY Why are you here?

SARAH I'm here for you.

LILLY You're here for me? That's a first.

SARAH You owe me something. That's why. I'm here to collect a debt.

LILLY I owe you something? I owe you *nothing*.

SARAH Come on Lils. Let's turn Dad.

Lights out.

ACT TWO

Lights up. SARAH *is sat on a chair staring at her iPhone. On the table is a bottle of wine and two glasses.* LILLY *is standing looking out to the audience. Inspecting herself in a mirror.*

LILLY Would you shag me?

SARAH I'm sorry?

LILLY Am I fuckable? Look at me. Am I fuckable? *(Beat)* Still? I worry I'm not massively fuckable.

SARAH Everyone's fuckable Lilly. It's all relative.

LILLY Relative?

SARAH Yes. I mean, there are some parts of Norfolk where a dog is fuckable.

LILLY Thank you. I feel a lot better.

SARAH Lilly. Seriously. You're very attractive for a woman with two children.

LILLY I don't like this mirror.

SARAH *stands up. She walks around the room with her phone in the air.* LILLY *pours herself a huge glass of wine.*

SARAH The signal in this place is terrible. Do you get signal? I haven't had any signal at all...

LILLY You have to drive to the bottom of the road. Use the landline.

SARAH Landline?! Seriously. This place. It's primitive. Primeval.

SARAH *starts shaking her phone as if that might help.*

I mean... How does...how does anyone live here? Seriously. How does anyone get anything done at all? What...what is the point of places like this?

Now stood on a chair. Screaming at her phone.

OH. COME. ON! FUCK! FUCK! *FUUUUUUCCCCKKKK!*

LILLY You're stressed. I can tell. I'm your sister.

SARAH Oh yes. Thank you Mystic Meg. Look. I just need to read my fucking emails. OK? You wouldn't understand...

LILLY Yes. It goes right over my head all this email business. I like dancing and making pretty pictures.

SARAH That's not what I meant. Give me a break, Lilly. OK?

Turning her wrath back to her phone.

OH THIS IS JUST... JESUS FUCKING *FUCK!*

LILLY I think it's sad that you can't go two minutes without checking your phone.

SARAH It's like a third world country out here. If it gets any worse Angelina Jolie will turn up and fucking adopt us.

Absolutely losing the plot.

AHHHHHHHHHHHH!

LILLY I've instigated a no phones rule at home. In the bedroom. Clive and I are trying to be more present with one another.

SARAH How very modern.

SARAH sits down next to LILLY. Throws her phone petulantly on the table.

Is it working? Is Clive a model of mindfulness?

LILLY No. He listens to his radio instead.

SARAH takes a fag out. LILLY shoots her a look. SARAH rolls her eyes, puts them away.

SARAH How's Clive coping with you being away?

LILLY Fine. I'd imagine.

SARAH He's not been in touch?

LILLY No. He's not like that.

SARAH Like what? A human being?

LILLY He's not very communicative. He's got Asperger's. *(Beat)* He shows his love in different ways.

SARAH Asperger's? I had no idea. Asperger's? As in, like, officially? Has he been diagnosed?

LILLY No. Not officially, no. I just know.

SARAH You can't just diagnose someone with Asperger's.

LILLY I'm very intuitive.

A pause.

SARAH How is Clive?

LILLY He's fine.

SARAH You don't talk about him. You haven't mentioned him all night.

LILLY So what?

SARAH Nothing. Just an observation.

LILLY Clive's great. You know. A good father.

SARAH A good father.

LILLY Yes.

SARAH That's good.

A pause that SARAH is happy to drag out.

LILLY It's not going to be fireworks all the time. Of course not. There's ups and downs. But he's a good man. Reliable. He helps out around the house.

SARAH Sounds magical.

LILLY You've never managed anything long term, have you Sarah? *(Beat)* Just an observation.

A pause.

SARAH *(standing up, bored)* What's in that? Over there? Have you looked?

LILLY All sorts.

> **SARAH** *opens a drawer in a cabinet.*

I wouldn't if...

SARAH Oh my god.

LILLY I told you.

SARAH I think I'm going to faint. Have you seen this?

> **SARAH** *pulls some plastic packaging out of the drawer.*

Condoms. *(Beat)* A whole drawer full of condoms.

LILLY I did see that, yes.

SARAH *A DRAWER FULL.* They're extra large! *(Beat)* No wonder Mum needed a hip replacement.

LILLY I'm pleased for him. That he's been enjoying a physical relationship. That he's being safe... Oh God! Do you remember when Dad gave us 'the talk'?

SARAH Before the 5th form disco? That remains the most embarrassing day of my life. And I've shat myself on the tube. Twice.

LILLY All the boys worshipped you at school. Do you remember? Well, they were scared of you. I think. But still. They'd follow you around. Enraptured. Hypnotised by your ambivalence. *(Beat)* I always looked at your confidence and wondered how you did it.

SARAH I wasn't confident. I didn't feel confident.

LILLY Confident people always say that. They don't know what it's like to not have it.

SARAH You weren't un-confident. You used to wear a poncho to school.

LILLY I couldn't look anyone in the eye. I spoke to the floor.

SARAH You were a late bloomer.

LILLY I was the clever one though. I had that. You were cool. But I was the clever one. You've got to give me that?

SARAH Terry Lyons.

LILLY Don't. Please. Don't.

SARAH Do you remember Terry Lyons?

LILLY Of course I remember him.

SARAH Terry Lyons! Never understood what you saw in him. He was a sigh in a tracksuit.

LILLY He was a bit wet.

SARAH He was sodden. Dripping.

LILLY Perhaps. But he had his own car.

SARAH That's not strictly true, is it. He was on the insurance for his Dad's Austin Allegro.

LILLY A car's a car.

SARAH All the doors were different colours. It had a child seat in the back.

LILLY And he had a job. Prospects.

SARAH He was a cobbler.

LILLY Nothing wrong with being a cobbler.

SARAH No one's a cobbler. Terry Lyons must have been Britain's only cobbler.

LILLY He was Britain's *youngest* cobbler. He used to boast about it.

SARAH He used to boast about it?

LILLY Look, he had a car, money to burn, a glint in his eye.

SARAH You make it sound like you were going out with Rick Astley.

LILLY Terry wasn't much of a catch. But he liked me. And he was kind. And that was enough.

SARAH He was weird! And spotty. And he smelt of polish.

LILLY Didn't stop you kissing him though did it?

A few beats of silence.

Second drawer from the top.

SARAH I'm not sure I want to look in any more drawers.

LILLY There's a treat for you. I promise.

SARAH *opens the drawer.*

SARAH Oh! RIM. THE. POPE. This is incredible.

SARAH *puts on a toupee. Johnny Cash, basically.*

What a rug! WHAT. A. SYRUP. He did not wear this, surely?! As in. Like. Wear it?

LILLY *(getting to her feet)* Afraid so. I found photographic evidence.

SARAH *(heavy cockney accent, Ray Winstone)* 'If you get pregnant girls, it's the end of your life. Just ask your mother.'

LILLY, *laughing, grabs the toupee off* SARAH's *head and puts it on instead.*

LILLY *(gyrating her hips like Elvis)* I'm all shook up. Un-huh-huh.

Beat.

SARAH *is doubled over.*

Look what else I found.

LILLY *grabs a boom box. Presses play. "YOU SEXY THING" by Hot Chocolate.**

SARAH Oh my god. Do you remember mum's 'sexy dancing'!

SARAH *does an impression, all erotic shoulder rolling and coquettish pouting.* **LILLY** *is in hysterics. She takes off the wig, then skips the track. Berlin, "TAKE MY BREATH AWAY".** When the vocal kicks in they both spontaneously break into a dance routine they remember. It's perfect and elaborate. Every move choreographed to be a literal representation of each lyric. They sing the chorus to one another. Then...*

Dad loved that song. Do you remember his fiftieth? He made everyone watch him do an acoustic version of it –

LILLY And then he had an asthma attack during the chorus! I should write that down, actually. That's good material for the eulogy...

LILLY *retrieves a notebook.*

SARAH That was your first dance. Dad was so proud.

LILLY For once.

SARAH Clive looked absolutely terrified...

LILLY He's not a dancer, Clive.

SARAH You looked so happy. So beautiful.

LILLY You'll meet someone one day.

A pause.

SARAH *(turning off the boom box)* I'm sick of this.

---

*/** A licence to produce *Kin* does not include a performance licence for "YOU SEXY THING" or "TAKE MY BREATH AWAY". For further information, please see Music Use Note on page v.

LILLY Of what?

SARAH Of being patronised. Smug couples. Implying singledom is some perverse eccentricity... A dreadful curse to be endured...

LILLY I wasn't...

SARAH Rather than what it is. A carefully considered choice. Of something better.

LILLY What have you chosen exactly?

SARAH To be alone. Free. To be 100% responsible for my own life –

LILLY You used to love people. When we were growing up. A real social butterfly –

SARAH Because I was 'the fun one'. I wasn't allowed to be shy –

LILLY You'd light up rooms. That's why I always looked at the floor. I was blinded –

SARAH I'd be wheeled out by Dad. Like some vaudeville act. We may have been treated equally, me and you. But we weren't treated the same.

LILLY Do you actually believe that's even possible? To be 100% responsible for your own life?

SARAH What if I don't want to meet someone? What if I prioritise other things? Like my career.

LILLY By which you mean money.

SARAH Money is part of it. Yes.

LILLY The biggest part of it. In the city.

SARAH So what? Money's a scorecard. That's all. I'm not obsessed with money.

LILLY But you want lots of it.

SARAH Because that's the game I'm playing. I like to win. Winning is fun.

LILLY I'm poor. Does that make me a loser?

SARAH No. Because you're playing a different game.

LILLY It doesn't feel like a game. Feels pretty real to me.

SARAH We all need a story to be the hero of. The people round here have God. You've got your family. I have money. *(Beat)* We all pick our delusion. Then we have the gall to look down on each other's.

LILLY I don't look down on you.

SARAH Was it ever fireworks? With Clive.

LILLY Well, there was no thunderbolt. If that's what you mean?

SARAH What was it then? Light drizzle?

LILLY Clive just sort of grew on me.

SARAH It was Stockholm syndrome.

LILLY Do you ever regret not having children? I do wonder sometimes how becoming a mother might have affected you. How you would have changed.

SARAH *laughs.*

What's funny?

SARAH Nothing.

LILLY You laughed. Why? Tell me. What's so funny?

SARAH I find it amusing, that's all. How superior you think you are. Because you're a mother.

LILLY I don't think I'm superior.

SARAH It baffles me that mothering is seen as this rarefied skill. Some celestial blessing. Rather than what it is. An instinct. Like eating or shitting.

LILLY Do you think it's easy being a mother?

SARAH I'm so sick of hearing about family. Of feeling guilty. For not enjoying family. Of being pressured into joining a standing ovation for a show I didn't particularly care for in the first place.

LILLY Money though. That's moral.

SARAH It's not immoral. I've earned my money. I deserve it.

LILLY If you say so.

SARAH Are you still making your jewellery?

LILLY What's that got to do with anything?

SARAH You were good. You were brilliant, actually. I still wear some of your stuff. Why not? Why did you stop?

A pause.

You had such potential.

LILLY Don't tell me what potential I had.

SARAH I saw it with my own eyes.

LILLY Potential's just a story other people tell about you. Based on what *they* see. On what *they* pay attention to. I've fulfilled my potential. Just in ways you don't value.

SARAH's *phone bleeps and vibrates loudly announcing her emails. She rushes to read them, panicked.*

Why did you kiss Terry?

SARAH *(distracted)* I don't know. It was an age ago. A different world –

LILLY But you remember it.

SARAH Yes. I remember it. It was like snogging a cod.

LILLY So why did you do it?

SARAH It's not important now –

LILLY Why did you kiss Terry?

SARAH I don't want to talk about it –

LILLY Why did you do it? *Why did you kiss Terry?*

SARAH Because you were being me and I didn't like it.

A pause.

Where are your keys?

LILLY On the side. Why?

SARAH I need to borrow them.

LILLY Now?

SARAH Yes. Now. I need to go for a drive.

LILLY Where?

SARAH To the end of the road.

LILLY Ok. Well maybe just wait till after lunch?

SARAH No. I need to go now.

LILLY Saz. Lunch is in the oven. Surely you can wait...

SARAH Lilly! I NEED TO GO NOW!

Blackout.

ACT THREE

Lights up. The two sisters are sitting next to each other around the table. There are a bunch of takeaway cartons. They've ordered far too much. SARAH *– chopsticks in hand – is eating noodles like a ravenous beast.* LILLY *– holding a baby monitor – is watching her, a little appalled.*

SARAH You've got to hand it to the Chinese...

LILLY I didn't understand a word of that.

SARAH You've got to hand it to the Chinese. Resilient people. You can be in the most remote, dingiest shit hole on the planet. And there will be a Chinese family somewhere. Banging out cartons of fried rice. I've got a lot of time for them.

LILLY Are you alright with those chopsticks? Or would you like me to fetch you a spade?

SARAH *shovels in another mouthful.*

SARAH What's that?

LILLY I need a translator...

SARAH *(pointing)* What's that?

LILLY It's a baby monitor. For Dad. So we can check his breathing.

LILLY *turns it on. They listen to the breathing for a few beats.* SARAH *starts to loudly hum the Darth Vader theme, for no more than four bars.*

Yes. Thank you, Sarah. Thank you for your helpful contribution.

SARAH *(as Darth Vader)* 'I am your father!'

LILLY Dad woke up when you went to the shops.

SARAH Why didn't you say anything?

LILLY He asked for you. He wanted to see you. You were always his favourite –

SARAH Stop saying that.

LILLY I made him some food. He wouldn't eat it. All he wanted was jelly and ice cream. He couldn't stop weeping. It was a pathetic sight, actually –

SARAH What did he say?

LILLY His hands were freezing. His feet have turned blue. But he complained of being hot. Like there was a fire in his stomach –

SARAH Lilly, for God's sake.

LILLY He wanted to talk about mum. He said he should never have left. That she was the only woman he ever loved. He was angry. Angry that he had ruined *his* life –

SARAH Did he say anything about me?

LILLY He made me promise that I'd look after you –

SARAH I don't need looking after.

LILLY I said that I would. I said I'd look after you –

SARAH I don't need looking after.

LILLY I can't stop thinking about it. About what he said. About Mum. There's no remorse. Just self-pity. It's still all about him.

SARAH Surely you can forgive a dying man being self-absorbed.

LILLY He's never said sorry –

SARAH We're making a big assumption in all this –

LILLY Never shown contrition –

SARAH We're assuming that what he did was morally wrong.

LILLY He walked out on his two daughters. On his depressed wife. To shack up with a younger woman on a different continent. I'd say that's pretty cut and dried –

SARAH I don't think it's cut and dried. Not at all –

LILLY I can't believe you're defending him –

SARAH Someone has to. I think he's been misunderstood.

LILLY Do you believe all these things you say? Sometimes I think you say them only for effect.

SARAH *stands up to pour herself a drink.*

SARAH We can't escape our biology. Our programming. It's invisible. But it's there.

LILLY That's what it was. Was it? A lion on the Savannah. Prowling. Spreading his seed. Come on. You're better than that.

SARAH I don't sleep well –

LILLY Indigestion is it?

SARAH I listen to a lot of podcasts. They help me pass the time... Did you know, there are three neurochemicals involved in love? Testosterone, oxytocin and dopamine.

LILLY We need to make a list of his passwords. I must do that.

SARAH Testosterone's responsible for lust. Oxytocin: attachment. Then it's dopamine's that makes you feel in love.

LILLY Love is a lot messier than that.

SARAH But dopamine wears off after two years. On average. It sticks around long enough for mates to reproduce. Wean the child. And then: kaput. Isn't that interesting?

LILLY Not really.

SARAH Love. *Love* is mendacious. It's presented as moral, pure. This end to which all things are aimed. Rather than what it is. A capricious chemical reaction. Wrapped inside a story of happily ever after.

LILLY Capricious. That's a long word. Well done.

SARAH So. The question is. If Dad fell out of love with mum. Is he morally responsible for leaving?

LILLY Of course he is –

SARAH Should a man, or indeed a woman – because a woman might be in this situation Lilly, let's not forget. Should a man stay with someone they don't love anymore? Should you stay in a relationship that makes you miserable?

LILLY It's got nothing to do with love. It's got everything to do with responsibility.

SARAH What about responsibility for yourself?

LILLY We're more than our biology. We're not simply another animal. Cocks and clits swaying on the breeze. We've got memories. Imaginations. We exist in the past. And future. And apart from that, we have a conscience. A fucking conscience. Right here, right now.

SARAH You don't owe anyone feelings –

LILLY Perhaps not. But you do owe them respect. Love –

SARAH You use the word love in a million different ways. It's meaningless –

LILLY It's not meaningless to me –

SARAH What if Dad was in love with the other woman? The American. Can I say her name? Or is that heresy?

LILLY If you're desperate to.

SARAH Charna. What if he was in love with beautiful, pert Charna? Does that not change things? Does love not trump duty? What's more life-affirming? What's more heroic?

LILLY Heroic! Heroic she says! What a word. What an interpretation –

SARAH Maybe Dad was brave. Maybe he just exercised his freedom. Rather than being afraid of it –

LILLY This is not about *him*. It's not about *his* life. It's about us. Me and you. It's about Mum. He ruined her life. Then you vanished and I was left to pick up the pieces—

SARAH That's not true –

LILLY You got bored and abandoned us. Just like Dad –

SARAH I didn't abandon you. I left. They're different things –

LILLY Mum was doing well. At last. She was happy. Christ, I'd go as far to say she was full of beans. Then bang. Dad announces he's leaving –

SARAH She enjoyed being the victim. That's the thing with martyrs –

LILLY Sixteen years of marriage thrown back in your face. Do you know what it takes? To sustain a marriage? Do you know how much sick you have to swallow to get through the troughs?

SARAH I had a life to lead. Ambitions. I had no choice –

LILLY He left *nothing*. Just an unpaid mortgage. And a hollowed out woman. The world blowing through her like an abandoned barn. Is that not what happened? Do you not remember that?

SARAH It was the negativity I couldn't stand. Sadness everywhere. Everything began to taste of it –

LILLY Do you have any idea what it took to get Mum moving again?

SARAH It was usually booze –

LILLY If you knew the effort. To get her up in the mornings. To open the curtains. To try and get her to see the sunshine. And not the vast, empty space in front of her. Another day of meaningless...*nothing*. She wouldn't eat. She wouldn't wash –

SARAH I wrote to her. I wrote to her every month –

LILLY Oh yes! Thank you! What a sacrifice! To scrawl two pages of A4 every few weeks. Not to mention the price of stamps. And then there's the walk to the post box. Which must have taken, what? Minutes? Whole minutes of your life.

SARAH I didn't like Mum. I didn't admire her. But I loved her. I loved mum.

LILLY Perhaps. But you loved her from a safe distance. I was at the coalface. Hands bloody. Face sweaty. By the messy grunt work of loving someone... And those letters. Those letters were the highlight of her month. She'd reread them. Again. And again. Until the next one arrived. This smile would take over her. Like she'd been transported somewhere else. Somewhere happier. Somewhere I wasn't... I'd watch her read your letters. Hear her talk about them. About how proud she was. About how *excited* she was. And I'd feel invisible. Like you'd made me disappear. And I'd hate her. And I'd hate you.

There's a rasping sound from the baby monitor. The girls hush immediately and gather around it. The breathing is heavy, uneven. And then: silence. The girls look terrified: has he stopped breathing? Then we hear a fart. And the breathing goes back to normal. **LILLY** *stands up and sits on the floor next to a pile of things she has been sorting out and continues with the task. A few beats pass.*

SARAH Your memory's playing tricks on you. You're myth making.

LILLY How would you know? You weren't there.

SARAH You've conveniently missed a bit.

LILLY You can't rewrite history. I won't let you.

SARAH I don't want to rewrite history. I just want it accurately recollected. You're missing a few, crucial years. Years that change everything –

LILLY You're drunk.

SARAH I left when I was nineteen. Dad disappeared three years before that –

LILLY I cared for Mum till she died –

SARAH I held the family together for as long as I could –

LILLY I can't believe I'm hearing this –

SARAH I lied for you. I took the rap for you. Again and again and again. You were a demon. A totally different person. Angry. At Dad. At Mum. At me. Anything to not feel sad –

LILLY Rubbish.

SARAH You'd disappear for days on end. Play truant from school. Hang out with those awful boys from the Acorn Estate. Fuck them. Boast to me about it. Do you not remember this? How have you forgotten this? Because I haven't. It's right there. Fresh as a wound. Mum screaming in my face when she'd found your drugs. I said they were mine. Because you were the good one. That's all you had –

LILLY That's not how it was. Not at all –

SARAH Stealing Mr Sampson's car. Do you remember that? His embarrassing BMW. Do you remember nicking it? Doing doughnuts on the rec. Wrapping it around a tree. I took the rap for you. Like everything else. Because you were my sister. Because one last thing and you'd be expelled. And the other school up the road didn't have an art department. I did it for you. Even though. Lilly. *The clever one. The brains.* Even though it cost me a fucking place at Cambridge.

LILLY I don't...

SARAH And do you remember the pond? The one Dad put in for their fifteenth anniversary? A carp for every year of marriage. Each a different colour. Do you remember those? They were beautiful. Mum loved them. After Dad left she'd put a rug down and just stare at them. It relaxed her –

LILLY *(standing)* Of course I remember –

SARAH Mum picked me up from school. I'd finished my final exam and we'd been out for pizza. We come back home. And there they were. Floating. You killed the fish! *You killed all the fish Lilly.* You killed Mum's fish! So don't talk to me about saving Mum. About being a firefighter. Don't you fucking dare say that. Because I may have fled a burning building. But you. YOU were the arsonist.

A pause.

LILLY You can hardly blame me. Can you? For acting up –

SARAH Acting up!

LILLY After what I'd been though –

SARAH We'd been through the *same thing.*

LILLY Maybe. But I always felt the world much more intensely than you did.

SARAH So you admit that you did those things? You accept it's the truth?

LILLY It doesn't *feel* true...

SARAH Truth has nothing to do with feelings. It has everything to do with facts.

LILLY What about the moral truth? What about what I *experienced.* I am the victim here.

SARAH You owe me a thank you.

LILLY You want me to *thank* you?!

SARAH I don't expect an apology. But I do want you to say thank you.

LILLY Oh thank you Sarah! Seriously. Thank you for missing my entire adult life. Thank you for leaving me with Mum. In the state she was in. Thank you for letting me organise the funeral. All by myself. Did you know I've had a miscarriage? That I've had breast cancer? I really am so grateful for everything. I don't know what I would have done without you –

SARAH *(grabbing* LILLY*'s clothes, screaming)* I want you to admit what you did –

LILLY This is disgusting. This is repugnant to me. Say thank you! You should be on your knees. Begging me. Begging me to forgive you. You should be fucking grovelling.

SARAH *(now a full-on physical fight)* SAY. THANK YOU!

Another rasping noise is heard on the baby monitor. Much louder this time. In the bedroom next door, an arm drops from the bed; smashing a glass of water smashing on to the floor. The girls rush into the room.

Blackout.

ACT FOUR

LILLY *is sitting behind the table, which is covered in papers.* SARAH *is in the other room. Hunched in a chair. Staring numbly at the body.*

LILLY *(on the phone)* About an hour ago... I'd say about ten past eleven... Of course. Keith Barnaby Chapman... 20 Somertown Drive... Zip code is 83176 ...It's at the end of a long road... there's, well, there's a sort of plastic Pingu thing... Pingu... Pingu... Pingu, yes...well he's a sort of a talking penguin... err it's not really in any language...he just sort of squawks... Listen. I don't really want to talk about it... Yes. Well. Err. What happens next? What does one do? ...Well he can't stay here... He's in the bedroom at the moment.... OK... Thank you... Well, looking forward to seeing you... Sorry. I don't know why I said that... Yes. Goodbye then.

LILLY *finishes speaking then breaks down in tears.* SARAH, *now stood by the door, watches her cry for a few moments, thinking. Then she goes into the bedroom and puts on her father's jacket. She gets the toupee out of the drawer, puts it on. She approaches her sister from behind.*

SARAH *(in her Dad's voice; leering)* Hello darlin'!

LILLY *jumps out of her skin. Leaping off the chair.*

LILLY Sarah! Fucking hell.

SARAH Sorry. I thought... I thought you could do with a laugh.

LILLY It's not funny.

SARAH It is quite funny.

LILLY *slowly breaks into giggles. As does* SARAH. *They look at each other for a few beats.*

He looks different now. Like something's left him. Vacant. Open mouthed. He doesn't look himself.

LILLY Yes he does. That's exactly how he looked when West Ham lost.

SARAH I was thinking. In there. What were his last words?

LILLY He was worried about that. You know? Said he'd put a lot of thought into them. He wanted them to be witty. Wise. A fitting epitaph...

SARAH What were they? In the end?

LILLY It was something about not liking onion.

A pause.

SARAH I didn't get the chance to say goodbye.

LILLY I thought you didn't care about dad? *(Beat)* I'm sure he was grateful you were here. You were his favourite.

SARAH That's not true.

LILLY I always knew that I wasn't what he wanted. But I had no idea what was wrong with me... I suppose I'd better hoover...

SARAH *takes off the toupee. Goes to sit down.*

The hospital are sending some people. Shouldn't be too long.

Walking off as if to do an errand.

I better put on some make-up... We need to speak to someone about the dog. Oh and Dad wanted his death announced in *The Times.* God knows why. He only ever read *The Sun.* But perhaps you could ring them?

SARAH This is everything. In this room. This is it. A whole life. Eighty-three years. It's pathetic. Isn't it? To reach the end and have just this?

LILLY He had friends. I'd imagine.

SARAH Then where are they now? I'm embarrassed. I'm embarrassed on his behalf.

LILLY We'll have to throw away all that cheese...

SARAH But what have I got? What would I leave? If I dropped dead now? If my plane ploughed into the Atlantic?

LILLY Sarah. You've got lots... You've got your health. Your career. A beautiful apartment. And you're thin. You're so fucking thin. It makes me furious.

SARAH I've got even less than him.

LILLY You've got me.

SARAH Do I?

A pause.

My emails came through in the end.

LILLY Really? Oh good. What a relief.

SARAH They waited till I left the country. And then they fucked me.

LILLY Who did? What are you talking about?

SARAH They waited for my Dad to die. And then they fucked me.

LILLY I'm lost. Frankly.

SARAH I've been sacked Lilly. With immediate effect.

LILLY What?

SARAH The emails.

LILLY Is this a joke? Are you joking?

SARAH No. But it's funny. Isn't it? To lose your father and your job on the same day. It's hilarious, actually.

LILLY I still don't know whether you're joking.

SARAH Libor. You probably don't know what that means, do you? Libor?

SARAH *lights a cigarette.*

It's interest rates – fixing interest rates. Derivatives— It's too boring to— We were stealing. Basically. That's the long and the short of it...

LILLY I'm not sure I can cope with this today –

SARAH We were all doing it. For decades. We always got away with it. No one cared. We were making money. Paying taxes. Well. Some taxes. Rising tide raises everyone's boats –

LILLY I'm too tired for this now.

SARAH Then – WHOOSH! – the financial crisis— Betty from Wolverhampton has her bungalow repossessed— suddenly we're criminals— I'm a criminal. ME. They pinned it all on me. All of them.

LILLY I'm sure it's just been a big misunderstanding –

SARAH I could go to prison.

LILLY You'll be able to explain all this away. You always could.

SARAH Not this time. I did it. I did all of it. But so did they. We were in it together. We were friends...

LILLY You were colleagues. It's not the same thing.

SARAH The others were exonerated by the board – said I was the ringleader. The ring leader! My boss was seventy-four years old. Seventy-four! He was old enough to be my...

LILLY Father.

A pause.

SARAH You know, he once told me that he viewed abortions as a business expense?

LILLY You had an abortion?

A pause.

SARAH *(darkly amused)* I put my boss down as my next of kin. Doesn't get much more depressing than that.

LILLY You could have called me. I would have dropped everything.

SARAH I wanted to do it alone.

LILLY It's not like you need to work. You could probably afford to never work again.

SARAH I haven't got any money.

LILLY You don't need to be coy Sarah. We're long past that.

SARAH All my bonuses. Most of my salary. Were tied up in share options.

LILLY Sell them then.

SARAH I've brought the company into disrepute. My claim to the shares. It's null and void. It's in my contract. It's all in my fucking contract. I gave my life to that place. Every single piece...

SARAH *stands up. Walks over to the mirror. Stares at it. Pulls at her face. Almost violently.*

LILLY You'll always have your apartment –

SARAH That fucking apartment. The vacuous opulence of it... I can see my face in almost every surface... It doesn't look like my face. Not anymore. But it's got my eyes. The ones you remember...

LILLY I always wanted your eyes. And your legs, actually.

SARAH You know. When Dad called me. He'd give me career advice.

LILLY You took career advice from Dad!

SARAH I didn't listen to it. But I played along. Played the part of the child so he could feel like a parent.

SARAH *approaches a bin bag on the floor. Picks it up. Empties it over the floor as she speaks.*

The last time he rang. He told me about his fishing. Said most days he'd wade out on the river. Catch salmon... apparently salmon return to the same place every year. To breed. They follow the scent trail. Right back to where they were born... I make the same mistakes. Again and again.

She picks a photo up. Looks at it.

Do you think I'm on the spectrum? Like Clive? Do you think I might be autistic?

LILLY Sarah. Please. Stop.

SARAH Then at least I'd have a label. For what I am. Something to explain it all away.

LILLY Explain what away?

SARAH I've run away from anyone who's ever loved me. *(Beat)* I look at you. At your instinct for love. At your appetite for it. And I am not sure I have it in me. I just don't feel it.

LILLY You used to.

SARAH Sometimes you've had a scar for so long. That you forget what caused it...

LILLY Let's have a cup of tea.

SARAH *(as* SARAH *speaks she picks up photos from the floor and cuts them with scissors)* Dad loved Polaroids didn't he... any excuse...that's us in the bath together look... Polaroids were perfect. For him. A fleeting moment of happiness. Captured. Then displayed forever. The lie that can never be rebutted...

LILLY Sarah. Please. You're scaring me.

SARAH If I could forget who I was. Then I wouldn't feel so bad for who I am...

LILLY *stops her cutting the photos. Takes her scissors away.*

It's just us left now. Hard to imagine. Isn't it? Those two little girls in the bath. We're orphans. Now Dad's gone. Nothing left in common.

LILLY Look on the floor. There are a hundred things we have in common.

SARAH *moves away from* **LILLY.**

SARAH Well. That's my turn out of the way. It's your go now. That's how it works. Isn't it? From memory. Truth or dare?

LILLY We're not playing a stupid game.

SARAH You used to love games. Come on! Truth or dare?

LILLY Don't be absurd.

SARAH Oh come on. It will cheer me up. Truth or dare?

LILLY No. Sarah.

SARAH Truth or dare?

LILLY *(exhausted)* Truth.

SARAH Are you in love with Clive?

LILLY Love isn't the same as being in love.

SARAH Do you love him?

LILLY No.

SARAH Well, well, well. Look at the state of us. What a pitiful mess. *(Beat)* We are what we are. I suppose. We're Chapmans.

SARAH *begins to take the foil off the champagne bottle.*

I don't sleep. I told you that. Didn't I? Not a surprise really. Given all the coke. But I do get a lot of reading done. So every cloud...

SARAH *pours two glasses of champagne. The dog starts barking.*

There's this story. About a man who falls asleep in a room. Then the room's locked so he can't leave. But he doesn't know. So when he wakes up, he think he's free to leave the room. But actually. He isn't. He isn't free at all. *(Beat)* We were always going to become them. Do you realise that? We were condemned to this. Doesn't that make you angry?

(brightly, carrying over the glasses) This *is* a celebration after all. I propose a toast. To the Chapmans. We look after our own, don't we? The Chapmans. Unless it's inconvenient.

SARAH *offers a flute to* LILLY *who looks at her, not taking the glass.* SARAH *unperturbed puts it down on the table in front of her.*

So raise your glasses please. To the Chapmans. A family. Or is it a terminal illness? Cheers.

SARAH *downs her glass.* LILLY *leaves hers untouched.* SARAH *moves to refill her glass.*

LILLY I was in the loft last week. I found a box. Full of our stuff. Toys. Dolls. All sorts. There were these costumes... Do you remember Tom March? From next door? He had an inhaler. He used to squeeze his willy when he needed a wee...

SARAH Tom March. He was six years old. But he looked like an old man.

LILLY He had a birthday. Tom and his brother were dressed as Batman and Robin. We were damsels in distress. Waiting to be rescued... But you got bored. And you chased Tom till he ran out of breath –

SARAH I tied him up. At the bottom of the garden –

LILLY You put on his Batman costume. Then I did the same to his brother. I became Robin. The boys started crying... Mum took us home. In disgrace. Do you remember? She went absolutely mad. Because we wouldn't stop laughing about it.

A short pause.

SARAH What happened to us?

Blackout.

ACT FIVE

Lights up. The body has been removed from the second room so the bed lies empty. In the other room LILLY *sits doing paperwork. Her glass of champagne remains untouched.* SARAH *appears from offstage.*

SARAH Come and have a look.

LILLY No.

SARAH Come and have a look.

LILLY Sarah. I am not having a look.

SARAH Please.

LILLY It's weird.

SARAH It's not weird. We're sisters.

LILLY I'm not doing it.

SARAH Please.

LILLY No.

SARAH Seriously. It's absolutely massive.

LILLY No.

SARAH You'll be impressed?

LILLY No. I am not having a look at your poo!

SARAH Oh go on. It's my biggest ever. *(Beat)* It looks like a horse's neck.

LILLY Good for you.

SARAH You used to love looking at my poos.

LILLY Yeah. When we were children. I'm forty-four.

SARAH Your loss.

SARAH disappears from view. We hear a flushing. A few beats. Then another flush.

(reappearing) I'll have another go in a minute.

SARAH sits in a chair next to LILLY. A few beats of silence.

I can't believe they dropped him. I even said, don't drop him. They looked at me like I was an idiot. And then they dropped him.

LILLY They were mortified. Bless them.

SARAH He didn't look too happy about it either. *(Beat)* Strange they brought an ambulance... But they're an optimistic bunch, aren't they? The Americans.

A pause.

I've ordered a cab by the way.

LILLY What?

SARAH I said –

LILLY You said you had to go. You didn't say you were going literally *now*.

SARAH It's just. My situation –

LILLY What about the funeral? What about the will?

SARAH Well I'm very happy for you to have his collection of beer mats if that makes things easier. *(Beat)* Thanks for taking care of everything...

A pause.

We'll have to fly him back. I suppose.

LILLY Well. I don't think Parcelforce will take him.

SARAH goes to put her hand on LILLY's knee. LILLY stands up.

I often ask myself why I killed those fish...

Moving over to the polaroids.

My whole life. Before Dad left. I was the good one. Then he walked out and I realised, it had no currency. Being good... It hadn't made him stay. So I became bad... Then when you left too... I could never be more exciting than you. But I could be kinder. So I put on my halo again...

Looking through them as she speaks.

I don't think you have any idea how lonely I've been. Without you. We had our own language... When you left. Part of me was amputated. You were my guts. You were my spine... That's how we survived. I leant on you. You leant on me. It's how we stayed upright...

SARAH I love you Lilly. You've all I got.

LILLY *(standing up again)* What a terrible reason to love someone. *Need.* It's the cheapest. The most fragile. How do you think that makes me feel?

SARAH You're not a consolation prize.

LILLY Maybe I bring it on myself. All of this. I do think that. Sometimes. That deep down. I don't want to be happy. Because being happy is bad. And misery is holy. Moral –

SARAH You sound like Mum.

LILLY At some point. The halo slipped down. Became a noose.

SARAH Kindness isn't a character flaw.

LILLY I can't do it anymore. I can't keep loving people who don't love me back.

LILLY *walks over to a bucket collecting drips from the ceiling. Looks at it.*

That leak's been there for ten years. 'I just never got round to fixing it,' he said. Drip. Drip. Drip. Drip. Drip. You know. You can be drowned by a drip if you wait long enough.

A short pause.

I'm going to leave Clive. I've decided. *(Beat)* Aren't you going to say anything?

SARAH What will your children think if you go?

LILLY What will my children think if I stay?

SARAH He was never right for you. You settled.

LILLY Everyone settles. It's the reason that matters. Do you settle because you want to build a life with this person. Or do you settle because you're afraid no-one else will want you...

SARAH What was your reason?

LILLY I think it's best that we don't see each other again. Either.

SARAH Lilly...

LILLY It's for the best.

SARAH Lilly please. Blood is thicker than water.

LILLY Maybe. But it's just as easy to pour away... Sammy asked me once. 'What is "death" mummy?' It's the sort of stupid question only a child can ask. Stupid. But brilliant. I'd actually never thought about it –

SARAH I'd like to meet Sammy. She sounds great –

LILLY Death is a mirror. And I don't like what I see. *(Beat)* My whole life I've given myself to other people. So tell me. After all you've done. Why should I give myself to you?

SARAH Because I'm your sister.

LILLY It's funny. Isn't it? That love is all we want. And yet we never pause to ask what love actually *is*...

SARAH It's a feeling. An instinct.

LILLY *(can't hide her disdain)* That's it. Is it? Love is biology.

SARAH You tell me then. Sounds like you're the expert.

LILLY I don't know what love is. But I know what it's not. It's not fear. It's not judgement. It's not worrying you're not enough. It's not punishment. It's not disgust. Or shame. Or betrayal. Or lies. Love…it's the opposite…

The ecstasy of love. Of being *in love*. The feeling of wanting to climb on the roof and scream at the fucking moon. Maybe. Yes. That's biological. But real love…

The love that lets a person be and become themselves. To feel they exist. And that they matter. THAT love isn't a feeling. It isn't biological. It's a verb. A set of things we do for one another. IT'S A FUCKING CHOICE. Sarah.

SARAH Do you love me? Lilly? Do you love me?

LILLY Honestly? No.

SARAH I love you.

LILLY No you don't. You don't really. You love me because I'm your sister. In that tepid, obligatory way. Because we just happened to have shared the same womb. But you don't LOVE. ME.

SARAH Lilly. You're breaking my heart.

LILLY Feels horrible. Doesn't it?

SARAH Lilly I'm sorry. I'm sorry for everything…

LILLY I can love you. I can do it again. But for me to love you, you need to love me. And it isn't words. It isn't a flimsy 'I love you.' It isn't a bottle of champagne. Or a pond full of carp. Love… It's fucking actions. I want you to be exhausted. Filthy. From the hard labour of loving me. Not on your time. But on mine. Not because of who I am. But despite who I am—

SARAH I want things to change—

LILLY Do you? Do you actually want it? Or will it just evaporate. As soon as you get home. As soon as something else comes along. As it always does. And you follow it. As you always do. Like a dog chasing a bubble—

SARAH *(tearful now)* I want to change. I really do—

LILLY Can you though? Can *you* change?

SARAH *(collapsing on her haunches)* I don't know. I don't know. I don't know.

Barely able to get her words out.

What if I'm destined to end up like him. Loveless. Friendless. Destitute. Totally unremembered.

LILLY *offers her a hankey. They sit together cross-legged on the floor.*

LILLY I did one of those DNA tests recently. Clive gave it to me as an anniversary present.

SARAH That's romantic.

LILLY He got me another present too.

SARAH Thank God for that.

LILLY It was a new Dyson.

SARAH Brilliant.

LILLY You can buy DNA tests online now. You spit into a vial and send it off. They analyse it in the lab. And tell you your ancestry.

SARAH I dread to think.

LILLY Our kin. It turns out. Half of them were from the Middle East. Originally. The other half were from Scandinavia. They were Vikings. Which explains your table manners.

SARAH And your cooking.

LILLY The Chapmans. Me and you. We're explorers. It's in our bones. We adapt. We change. It's who we are...

A few beats. SARAH *leans her head on her sister.*

When you have children. You realise. We aren't born fearful. We learn it...

SARAH I'm sorry. For what I did. For taking you for granted. Lilly. Please. I'm sorry. *(Beat)* Do you accept that? Do you forgive me?

LILLY Whenever people ask me about my family. I don't talk about you. I miss having a sister. I miss you so much.

We feel they might hug. Then the taxi hoots loudly.

That was quick. That's not like them.

SARAH I don't want to go.

The taxi hoots again. Louder and more often now.

LILLY Come on. You'll miss your flight.

SARAH *(rushed, standing)* I better flush the toilet. Please. Take the cash out of my purse. I owe you for so much...

LILLY I don't want your money.

SARAH Please. You've paid for everything.

LILLY Sarah...

SARAH I insist. It's on the side...

SARAH *disappears. We hear a toilet flushing. Meanwhile* LILLY *looks in* SARAH's *purse and finds a photo.* SARAH *returns. Notices. A beat.* LILLY *goes to hug* SARAH, *they are about to embrace when...*

LILLY Oh fuck. Fuck. Fuck. Fuck!

SARAH What?

LILLY The dog! I haven't fed the dog for hours. He must be starving.

LILLY *exits the stage. Then returns quickly.*

The dog's gone.

SARAH What do you mean? It's gone?

LILLY The back door's open. It's escaped.

SARAH rushes to the door. Next to LILLY.

SARAH Good for him.

The taxi hoots manically.

I really don't want to go.

LILLY It's fine. Come on.

They walk to the door.

SARAH Will I see you again?

LILLY I hope so. *(Beat)* But that's up to you.

SARAH I'll set up a WhatsApp group.

LILLY Oh no. Not another fucking WhatsApp group!

SARAH I love you.

They hug at last.

LILLY Thank you. For what you did. For me.

SARAH Goodbye.

LILLY Goodbye.

SARAH leaves. The door shuts.

I love you too.

*LILLY picks up her champagne. Moves to the boom box.
Music begins to explode out. She downs her champagne.
Blackout.*

The End

PROPS LIST

Chairs x6
Large table
Boxes SL (with condoms, toupee, scotch)
Pedestal SR with cactus
Carpet
Bin bag filled w. Polaroids and snaps
Scissors
SARAH's luggage
SARAH small handbag
Brick of duty free fags
Packet of fags and lighter
Bottle of champagne
Duty free bag
Bottle of wine
Bottle of scotch / bourbon
2 wine glasses
2 champagne flutes
1 tumbler
1 water glass
Chinese takeaway (US-style white boxes) w. cutlery, napkins etc.
Toupee
XL condoms
Paperwork (insurance forms etc.)
Baby monitor
Cassette player

LIGHTING EFFECTS

There's one state in the room. Using gobos, we made the light of
the day move around it. The start times of the acts are roughly
as follows: Act 1: 11a.m./late morning; Act 2: 2–3p.m.; Act 3:
10p.m.; Act 4: 1a.m., Act 5: 2–3a.m. Which means only the first
two acts are in daylight. Thus the state stays mainly the same
for Acts 3–5. Other than that there's an atmospheric pre-set;
perhaps highlighting some of the dad's artefacts on the set. And
a dipped state for the resets between acts.

SOUND EFFECTS

Preshow

A mix of mid-Western American radio stations: ads, jingles, clips of songs, shock jocks, static and tuning sounds. It needs to last about 7–10 minutes. The aim is to establish a sense of place by having it like scrawling along a radio dial in America. The songs should ideally be eighties stuff.

Act 1

There are no sound cues in Act 1. But there will be music during the blackouts to cover scene changes, including between Act 1 and Act 2. The tracks you choose need mixing in with other sounds of US radio chatter/interference etc. so they all inhabit the same world as the pre-show and the post-show.

Act 2

Hot Chocolate 'You Sexy Thing'/Berlin 'Take My Breath Away' cassette player tracks.
iPhone beeps and vibrations announcing SARAH's emails.

Act 3

Baby monitor sounds 1.
Baby monitor sounds 2.
Baby monitor sounds 3.
Glass smash sound effect.

Act 4

Dog barking sound effect.

Act 5

Two toilet flushes, sounding slightly different.
Taxi horn noises 1, 2 and 3. Increasingly strident.
Another toilet flush, again slightly different from the first two.

www.ingramcontent.com/pod-product-compliance
Lightning Source LLC
LaVergne TN
LVHW051802080426

835511LV00018B/3389